cat wisdom

to lift your spirits and brighten your day

BLUE ANGEL GALLERY
AUSTRALIA

Cat Wisdom: To Lift Your Spirits and Brighten Your Day

Published by Blue Angel Gallery, Australia
80 Glen Tower Drive
Glen Waverley, Victoria, Australia 3150
Phone: +61 3 9574 7776   Fax: +61 3 9574 7772
E-mail: tonicarmine@optusnet.com.au
Visit our website at: www.tonicarminesalerno.com

Writing by Tanya Graham
Photographs © Jane Burton / Warren Photographic
Concept by Toni Carmine Salerno

Design by Kiddie Punk Graphics

ISBN: 0-9757683-0-1

Cat Wisdom combines a set of brilliantly-shot and adorable photographs of kittens of all sizes and breeds with a collection of uplifting messages inspired by the inner wisdom of the cat world.

The photographs capture the true essence of the cat – playful, curious, intelligent, determined and stress-free.

The messages provide insight into your life from a cat's perspective, encouraging you to take life less seriously, to be proactive and enthusiastic, to explore new possibilities and opportunities, to express your feelings honestly without worrying what others may think and to take heart that your life is unfolding exactly as it needs to.

You are invited to share in the wisdom of these gorgeous kittens whenever you feel the urge!

introduction

Have the

courage

to do what you know is right.

Move forward with confidence

knowing that there are no mistakes,

only experiences

from which to learn and grow.

Pay special attention to what you are putting into your body. A **well-balanced diet** is the key to feeling healthy and having the energy you need to reach your potential each day.

Appreciate your family –

they are a source of unconditional love

and guidance to which you can

turn whenever you need advice.

Be clear about your purpose.

What are you setting out to achieve?

You will succeed only if you

remain 100% focused

on the goal.

Take a

closer look

at this situation

before you decide

how to act.

Things may not be

exactly as they

first appeared.

Make it clear where you stand

on this issue

and hold your ground.

It's important to let people know

when they are stepping

into your territory.

stand your ground

Now is a great time to start new projects.

Your mind will soon be filled with countless

new ideas and possibilities.

Wake up and embrace this time of action

and progress.

wake
up
and
get
started

Think outside the square

and you will unlock your

unique potential. Be a

leader, not a follower –

dare to be
different!

If you are feeling torn

about which direction to take,

it is time to make a decision.

Both paths will be

challenging and rewarding,

so choose one

and trust that whichever one

you choose will be the right one

for you.

It's time to move forward.

The gift of giving is a gift that gives back:

we often receive just as much by giving

as the person to whom we give. But be careful not to give

so much of yourself that there is nothing left for you –

you'll be left feeling drained and lacking energy.

There is a time for action and a

time for patience.

You have put in the hard work,

now there is nothing left to do but wait.

When the timing is right

you will start to see results

and your hard work will pay off.

speak your truth

Each of us has our own truth which is valid for us.

Feel free to sing your song and stand firm in your truth.

Don't be swayed by others,

but at the same time be sure to allow them to

voice their own opinions.

It's a time of action –

you will be able to achieve a great deal

if you act on the ideas and thoughts

that have recently come to you.

Approach life with confidence and determination –

nothing can stop you from reaching your goals.

An unlikely

friendship

is about to blossom

and will bring unexpected laughter

and joy into your life.

Be open to meeting new people

and remember to just be yourself.

You are seeking

a sense of security

and protection.

Trust that you are safe and look inside

yourself to find the courage to move forward

despite your fears.

If something has set off alarm bells for you recently,

be sure to follow your instinct.

You need to proceed with care.

If it doesn't feel right for you, trust your intuition and

be prepared to change your plans.

You are capable of so much more than you believe.

Challenge yourself to be the best that you can be.

Dare to push the limits and

discover

your

true

potential.

Welcome new opportunities

into your life

with

open arms.

There is no need to fear,

you are ready to learn something new.

Go out and explore your options

with an open heart and mind.

Since things have turned out the way they have,

you've probably been feeling a little startled and bewildered.

Not sure where to go from here?

don't panic. You just need to adjust your

original plan to accommodate this new revelation

and things will work out fine, it just may take

a little longer than you first thought.

You are moving in the right direction

but be aware that you need to

proceed with care.

Consider each step carefully

and

avoid

making impulsive decisions.

Make time

for
playtime.

Taking life seriously

all the time

leads to

unnecessary

stress

and

tension.

Instead remember to enjoy life

and be silly sometimes.

At times you may feel as though

everyone

around

you

is

different

to

you.

Learn to see differences in a more positive light.

Diversity keeps life interesting – embrace it.

Celebrate your

individuality.

You are the unique product

of your environment

and experiences.

Be proud of who you are!

It's only natural to be afraid

when faced with a difficult decision

or a new obstacle.

Try to calm your mind

by doing something relaxing

and the fear will soon subside.

You may have recently been feeling overwhelmed by the need

to keep **control** over different aspects of your life.

Try letting go of control and seeing where the river of life takes you.

You will still end up where you need to be, only the journey will

be much easier.

It's important to have dreams –

they give life direction and meaning.

Reflect on your **dreams** for your own life.

What is it that you truly desire?

The clearer you are about your dreams,

the easier it is to make them a reality.

You are ready to step up

to the next challenge.

Be confident in your

ability to emerge from

this next set of experiences

feeling enriched and

passionate about life.

What are you hiding from?

You have everything

you need

to deal with the situation that has presented itself,

there is no need for hesitation.

Life's journey is full of strange new encounters –

it's normal to feel a little bewildered by

an unexpected outcome or discovery.

Know that you are always equipped to deal

with whatever happens, so relax and

try to take life as it comes.

bewilderment

It's safe for you

to come out of hiding –

the coast is clear.

safety

You may feel as if you are

wandering into unfamiliar territory.

There's no need to be scared –

remember, life never throws you

more than you can manage.

While it is important to speak your truth and express your own

opinions, it is also necessary to allow others the same freedom.

Be tolerant of other people's views and be prepared to

reach

a compromise.

tolerance

acceptance

Love and accept yourself just as you are.

Nothing in your life needs to be fixed;

every aspect of you serves a purpose.

Just learn to accept that things are perfect just the way they are.

For many hundreds of years scientists and scholars

have been trying to work out how our world works,

and yet, the world remains full of mystery.

Instead of trying to figure everything out logically,

accept that some things will always be a mystery.

keep a lookout

An opportunity is coming your way

but you will need to be alert and attentive

if you are to recognise it.

You'll need to get in early to maximize its potential.

Keep your eyes peeled and your ears up.

Cats are renowned for their **curiosity** – the moment

they discover something new, it captures their attention and

they want to know everything there is to know about it.

Take a leaf out of the cat's book and explore the world

around you – your life will be more satisfying and rewarding for it.

Reflect on what you

have accomplished

to date.

Remember what

you were like five

years ago –

looking back you'll

realise just how far

you've come.

reflection

Acknowledge that

every single one of

your experiences

has helped you to

get where you are

and has served you

in some way.

Express

your feelings

and your creativity

will blossom. Everything

you feel is valid so let it all

out – good, bad, beautiful, ugly.

By expressing what's on your mind,

you will clear the way for new ideas to enter.

There is a **surprise** coming your way

which will change the way you look at life.

There is always room for a little cheekiness –

it helps people to lighten up and keeps life fun.

You need to be

flexible

in your approach to the

obstacle

you are facing.

Look at the situation

from every

possible perspective

and you will discover a

simple solution.

At times we move through life confidently with clear direction and purpose. At other times we have countless questions and are filled with a sense of doubt. Doubt creeps into our minds to encourage us to reflect on the choices we are making. Use this time to question some of your ideas and beliefs. You will come out of this period with more direction and focus.

strength in numbers

If you are feeling weak or afraid,

try calling on a friend

for company and support.

Together you will get through

this challenging time.

Great peace can be found in solitude.

Set aside some time each day,

even if it's only five minutes, to be alone.

You will calm your mind and attain a new sense of clarity.

the end

dog wisdom

to lift your spirits and brighten your day

dog wisdom book

Dog Wisdom is a collection of photographs and puppy-inspired words of wisdom which will encourage you to lead a more relaxed and happy lifestyle. Adopting some of the wise words of these gorgeous puppies will inspire you to have more fun, stay positive, allow you to give and receive more love, help you rediscover the joys of friendship and togetherness, give you a greater understanding of yourself and those around you and inspire you to pursue your dreams. A source of guidance and simple wisdom inspired by man's best friend!

dog wisdom & cat wisdom card sets

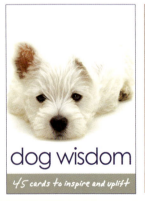

dog wisdom

45 cards to inspire and uplift

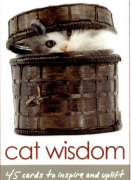

cat wisdom

45 cards to inspire and uplift

Now you can take the wisdom of man's best friends with you wherever you go with these fun and inspiring card sets. Using the 45 cards & accompanying guidebooks, the Cat Wisdom & Dog Wisdom cards allow you to easily and quickly receive uplifting messages everyday.

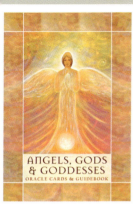

angels, gods and goddesses

Receive daily guidance from the Angels, Gods and Goddesses with this inspirational and accurate card set. Think of a question and then pick one or more cards to see what messages the oracle offers you today.

Features 45 cards & 64 page guidebook packaged in a hard cover box.

crystal oracle

This beautifully presented set of guidance cards featuring crystals, gems & minerals with an easy-to-use guidebook is designed to inspire and heal you as you connect to the profound love and wisdom which stem from the heart of the Earth.

Features 44 cards & 88 page guidebook packaged in a hard cover box.

spirit oracle

Give your spirit a voice! Ask a question, pick a card and listen to the guidance that stems from your own soul. Rediscover the magical and healing power of love that lies within you.

Features 54 guidance cards packaged in a hard cover box.

magdalene oracle

An eternal ocean of loving guidance. This inspirational and insightful card set will allow you to receive clear messages and give accurate readings for yourself and others. Featuring all new paintings, by artist Toni Carmine Salerno, the Magdalene Oracle is a tool you will use again and again.

Features 45 cards and guidebook packaged in a hard cover box.

universal wisdom

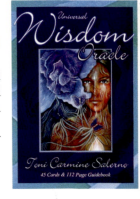

Universal Wisdom Oracle Cards will help bring clarity, peace and greater purpose into your life. Be divinely guided along your spiritual journey and inspired to create more love in our world.

Features 45 cards & 112 page guidebook packaged in a hard cover box.

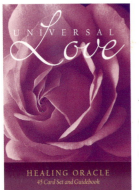

universal love

The Universal Love Healing Oracle will help bring clarity to specific questions. The guidebook offers interpretations, but pay particular attention to the images as they are able to convey what words cannot express.

Features 45 cards and guidebook packaged in a boxed set.

guardian angel cards

Guardian Angels are the messengers of light whose divine mission is to protect and guide humanity along its sacred journey.
Receive daily inspiration from your Guardian Angels by selecting one or more cards with a question in mind.

Features 46 heart-shaped cards packaged in a hard cover box.

lovers oracle

Featuring evocative messages to inspire love, the Lovers Oracle can be used for guidance on how to handle your most intimate relationships.

Features 44 heart-shaped cards in a hard cover heart-shaped box.

For more information please visit our website at:
www.tonicarminesalerno.com

blank journals

DREAM JOURNAL

GOLDEN MEMORIES JOURNAL

MEDITATIONS JOURNAL

INSPIRATIONS JOURNAL

REFLECTIONS JOURNAL

All journals (featuring the inspirational artwork of artist Toni Carmine Salerno on the covers) feature faint-lined pages enclosed in covered spiral binding. 160 pages. Page size: 6" x 8-1/4"

meditation CDs

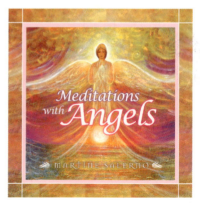

MEDITATIONS FOR INNER PEACE
by Toni Carmine Salerno

MEDITATIONS WITH ANGELS
by Martine Salerno